First Time

First Time 123

Melinda Beth Radabaugh

Heinemann Library

Chicago, Illinois

© 2004 Heinemann Library
a division of Reed Elsevier Inc.
Chicago, Illinois

Customer Service 888-454-2279
Visit our website at www.heinemannlibrary.com

Designed by Sue Emerson, Heinemann Library; Page layout by Que-Net Media™
Printed and bound in the United States by Lake Book Manufacturing, Inc.
Photo research by Janet Lankford-Moran

08 07 06 05 04
10 9 8 7 6 5 4 3 2 1

Library of Congress Cataloging-in-Publication Data
Radabaugh, Melinda Beth.
  First time 123/Melinda Beth Radabaugh.
      p. cm. – (First time)
Includes index.
Summary: From the first day Sunday to the seventh day Saturday, a child encounters new experiences, such as going to the doctor and getting a haircut.
  ISBN 1-4034-3869-2 (HC), 1-4034-3884-6 (Pbk.)
  1. Counting–Juvenile literature. [1. Counting. 2. Days.] I. Title: First time one, two, three. II. Title: First time 1 2 3. III. Title. IV. Series.
  QA113.R25 2003
  513.2'11–dc21

                                2002155335

Acknowledgments
The author and publishers are grateful to the following for permission to reproduce copyright material:
pp. 5, 23 Robert Lifson/Heinemann Library; pp. 7, 24 Image Bank/Getty Images; pp. 9, 11 Brian Warling Studios/Heinemann Library; p. 13 Mug Shots/Corbis; p. 15 Greg Williams/Heinemann Library; p. 17 Taxi/Getty Images; p. 19 Jeff Greenberg/PhotoEdit Inc.; p. 21 Rudi VonBriel/PhotoEdit Inc.; p. 22 (row 1, L-R) Brian Warling Studios/Heinemann Library, Image Bank/Getty Images; (row 2) Greg Williams/Heinemann Library; back cover (L-R) Brian Warling Studios/ Heinemann Library, Greg Williams/Heinemann Library

Cover photographs by (L-R) Brian Warling Studios/Heinemann Library, Robert Lifson/Heinemann Library, Greg Williams/Heinemann Library

Every effort has been made to contact copyright holders of any material reproduced in this book. Any omissions will be rectified in subsequent printings if notice is given to the publisher.

Special thanks to our advisory panel for their help in the preparation of this book:

Alice Bethke, Library Consultant
Palo Alto, CA

Eileen Day, Preschool Teacher
Chicago, IL

Kathleen Gilbert,
Second Grade Teacher
Round Rock, TX

Sandra Gilbert,
Library Media Specialist
Fiest Elementary School
Houston, TX

Jan Gobeille,
Kindergarten Teacher
Garfield Elementary
Oakland, CA

Angela Leeper,
Educational Consultant
Wake Forest, NC

Some words are shown in bold, **like this.**
You can find them in the picture glossary on page 23.

SEPTEMBER						
Sunday	Monday	Tuesday	Wednesday	Thursday	Friday	Saturday
1	2	3	4	5	6	7
8	9	10	11	12	13	14
15	16	17	18	19	20	21
22	23	24	25	26	27	28
29	30					

A **week** is seven days.

The days of the week are Sunday, Monday, Tuesday, Wednesday, Thursday, Friday, and Saturday.

A **calendar** shows the days of the **week**.

What will you do this week?

First 1st

The first day is Sunday.

You can go to a restaurant with your family.

Sunday	Monday	Tuesday	Wednesday	Thursday	Friday	Saturday
1	2	3	4	5	6	7

Second   2nd

The second day is Monday.

You can go to school on
a school bus.

Sunday	Monday	Tuesday	Wednesday	Thursday	Friday	Saturday
1	2	3	4	5	6	7

Third   3rd

The third day is Tuesday.

You can go to the library.

Sunday	Monday	Tuesday	Wednesday	Thursday	Friday	Saturday
1	2	3	4	5	6	7

Fourth   4th

The fourth day is Wednesday.

You can go to the doctor's **office** for a checkup.

Sunday	Monday	Tuesday	Wednesday	Thursday	Friday	Saturday
1	2	3	4	5	6	7

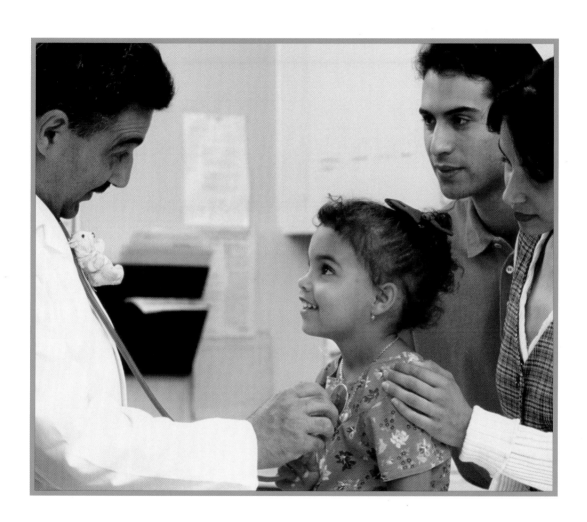

Fifth   5th

The fifth day is Thursday.

You can go the barbershop
for a haircut.

Sunday	Monday	Tuesday	Wednesday	Thursday	Friday	Saturday
1	2	3	4	5	6	7

Sixth   6th

The sixth day is Friday.

You can go to the dentist's **office.**

Sunday	Monday	Tuesday	Wednesday	Thursday	Friday	Saturday
1	2	3	4	5	6	7

Seventh 7th

The seventh day is Saturday.

You can fly in an airplane.

Sunday	Monday	Tuesday	Wednesday	Thursday	Friday	Saturday
1	2	3	4	5	6	7

What will you do next **week?**

You might try something new!

Quiz

Which thing did you do first?

Look for the answer on page 24.

Picture Glossary

calendar
page 4

office
pages 12, 16

week
pages 3, 4, 20

Note to Parents and Teachers

Learning ordinal numbers is a basic math skill. *First Time 123* helps children learn sequencing with ordinal numbers using days of the week as examples. You can help children make ordinal numbers a part of their math vocabulary by making them a part of your everyday talk. For example, as children line up to go outside you might ask them to tell you who is first in line, who is second, and so on. Alternatively, you could ask children to help you put groceries away at home. You might give them instructions to put the bananas away first, the apples second, the pears third, and so on.

Index

airplane 18

barbershop 14

bus 8

calendar 4

checkup 12

dentist 16

doctor 12

Friday 3, 16

haircut 14

library 10

Monday 3, 8

office 12, 16

restaurant 6

Saturday 3, 18

school 8

Sunday 3, 6

Thursday 3, 14

Tuesday 3, 10

Wednesday 3, 12

week 3, 4, 20

Answer to quiz on page 22

You went to a restaurant first.